Victory & Success Are Yours

by
JERRY SAVELLE

10th Printing
Over 95,000 in Print

Victory and Success Are Yours!
ISBN 0-89274-236-4
Copyright © 1982 by Jerry Savelle
P. 0. Box 748
Crowley, Texas 76036

Published by Jerry Savelle Ministries International
P. 0. Box 748
Crowley, Texas 76036

Victory and Success
Are Yours!

Success Is Conditional

Webster's New Collegiate Dictionary defines *prerequisite* as "something that is necessary to an end or to the carrying out of a function." Even though God's will is that you be fruitful, blessed, healed, and prosperous, there are some prerequisites to obtaining these things. There is something you must do or a condition you must meet. In this book we will discuss these prerequisites.

The promises of God are for His people. But that doesn't necessarily mean that they will automatically come to pass in your life. *You must meet the conditions.*

You might say to me, "When you start talking about conditions, you are talking about getting back under the Law."

3

No, I'm not! The Bible says in Hebrews 6:11-15 that we are to show forth the same diligence as our father Abraham. Nowhere in the Word of God will you find any statement suggesting that you can lie around doing absolutely nothing and expect God to bless you. In fact, God tells us that if we do nothing we will not succeed. Proverbs 6:10,11 and 24:33,34 emphasize that fact:

Yet a little sleep, a little slumber, a little folding of the hands to sleep: So shall thy poverty come as one that travelleth; and thy want as an armed man.

Use God's Spiritual Laws

The Word of God is spiritual law. God's Word is the perfect law of liberty (James 1:22-25). Once you begin to see these laws in the Word of God and to put them into effect in your life, they will produce the desired results. For instance, God's Word tells us how to achieve success. It says:

This book of the law shall not depart out of your mouth, but you shall meditate on it day and night, that you may observe and do according to all that is written in it; for then you shall make your way prosperous, and then you shall deal wisely and have good success (Josh. 1:8 AMP).

The spiritual law in the above verse is simply this: *Talking the Word + Meditating the Word + Acting on the Word = Prosperity, Dealing Wisely, and Success.* I have used this spiritual law in my personal life and ministry, and it has brought about great results.

Four Prerequisites To Victory

1. Decision - *Make a decision to win.* The Spirit of God said this to me: "Son, if you are not willing to make a decision to win, then you are not going to win." Success begins with your decision to succeed.

2. Determination - *Be determined to back your decision to win.* Many people make a decision to succeed without being determined to back that decision. Once you decide to win, you are making an unwavering commitment.

3. Discipline - *Discipline yourself to do only what the Word says and to say only what the Word says about every situation.* You cannot be moved by what you see, feel, or hear.

4. Diligence - *Always make a steady, consistent effort to accomplish your goal. Never give up.*

Decision and Determination

In John 5:1-9 we read an account of a man who had an infirmity for thirty-eight years. This man was in the midst of a multitude of people who were withered, halt, blind, and lame. In fact, society had called these people *hopeless cases.* Today medical science would write them off as *incurable.*

The man described in this passage had a *defeat image* in his heart. He had formed that image after being sick for thirty-eight years. Out of the abundance of this man's heart, his mouth spoke *defeat* (Luke 6:45). When Jesus asked him, *Wilt thou be made whole?* he spoke from the abundance of his heart and said:

"I am a cripple. I can't get up by myself and get into that pool. I don't have anybody to help me. Every time I try to get into the pool, somebody steps in before me."

The phrases *hopeless, incurable, no way out, beyond repair,* and *too far gone* are not in Jesus' vocabulary. Jesus was in the middle of those "hopeless cases" right where He wanted to be.

He began dealing with this man with the defeat image; and after He ministered to him, the man was made whole. But first the man had to make a decision to be made whole. When Jesus asked him, *Wilt thou be made whole?* He was demanding a decision from him. Wholeness was available to the man; but as long as he sat there without making a decision to receive it, he never would have been made whole.

Decide to Win

Man has a will. He has the right to make decisions. By his own will, he chooses God. God doesn't force man to choose Him. It is man's decision. As Kenneth Copeland says, "You can go to hell if you want to, and God will protect your right to go." But you don't have to go to hell if you'll make the decision to allow Jesus to become Lord of your life.

God puts it this way: *I call heaven and earth to record this day against you, that I have set before you life and death, blessing and cursing: therefore choose life, that both thou and thy seed may live* (Deuteronomy 30:19).

God said, "Here is life and blessing, and here is death and cursing. What is your choice?" It is your decision. You can have life and blessings or you can have death and cursing.

Whose decision is it to have life? *Yours.*

Whose decision is it for you to prosper? *Yours.*

Whose decision is it for you to be in health? *Yours.*

When Jesus said to the man, *Wilt thou be made whole?* He was telling the man that *the prerequisite to being made whole is to make a decision to be made whole.*

Jesus is *the same yesterday, and today and for ever* (Hebrews 13:8). The question that Jesus asked in His day is still the heart cry of Jesus to humanity today. He is still asking:

"Wilt thou be made whole? Wilt thou live above the beggarly elements of this world? Wilt thou be redeemed? Wilt thou be in health? Wilt thou prosper? Wilt thou be fruitful? Wilt thou be blessed?"

It is *your* decision! Jesus is saying, "I have already made it available. What I want to know is, will you have it?"

Wholeness hinges on your decision.

Christians have had the idea for too long that our healing is up to God only. We have prayed, "Heal us if it be Thy will." We thought if we squalled and bawled and talked "religious" that God would feel sorry for us, finally, and might give us about half of what we needed.

All this time God has been standing at the throne saying, "Come boldly and obtain all these love gifts that I have for you. Wilt thou live in health? Wilt thou prosper? Wilt thou be above and not beneath? Wilt thou be the head and not the tail? Wilt thou be blessed? Wilt thou have life? Wilt thou have all of thy household saved? Wilt thou have them all filled with the Holy Ghost? Wilt thou be what I have said in My Word that you can be? Wilt thou have great success?

God wants you to be made whole: spirit, soul, and body. Whether you will depends upon your decision.

Know the Facts

Many Christians spend all their time bombarding the gates of heaven when all the blessings are in the throne room and theirs for the taking. They have been outside rattling the gates while God is standing inside saying, "Aren't you going to come in?"

They've been saying, "I'm such a worm. I don't deserve to enter into the throne room. I don't deserve those love gifts." The sad part is that these people continue living defeated lives without knowing that they have a right to win.

Remember: Victory and success depends, first of all, upon the decision you make to win. As long as you think that you don't have a right to win and keep saying, "Whatever will be, will be," you will not enjoy victory or success.

You must base your decision to win upon facts. You must know that God says you can win.

The Bible says that you are the righteousness of God (2 Corinthians 5:21). You have a right to God's blessings. You don't deserve them on your own merit: *You deserve them on the merit of Jesus Christ.* He made you worthy.

The Bible says, *Delight yourself also in the Lord; and he shall give thee the desires of thine heart* (Psalm 37:4). When you delight yourself in the Lord, then your desires become His desires. You will never desire anything out of lust of the flesh, or out of anything that is damaging or destructive. You will only want what God desires for you.

Once you know what God desires for your life, then you will have solid ground upon which to stand.

Satan would love to keep you from getting what is rightfully yours. He accomplishes this through deception. If he can deceive you into believing that it's not God's will for you to win, then you won't resist his attacks.

One of the greatest revelations you could ever receive is: God's Word is His will. If you know what God's Word says, then you know what His will is. Don't *assume* that you have the facts; meditate the Word day and night until you *know* that you have the facts.

In order to get victory and success in any area of your life, you need to find out what the Word of God says about that particular area. Once you learn what the Word says, you have to make an unwavering decision, one on which you could base your life - to live according to the Word of God.

You can base your life on the Word because, as Jesus said, "God's Word is truth" (John 17:17). Truth is the highest form of reality that exists.

Many people say, "Just as soon as my finances get a little better, I am going to start giving to God." No! No! No! Don't wait until the circumstances change. Start giving now! In Luke 6:38 Jesus stated another of God's spiritual laws. He said, *Give, and it shall be given unto you.* When you start giving, your finances will change. If you keep putting off living by the Word until things look better, the Devil will see to it that they never do!

When the question is asked, *Wilt thou be made whole?* Lift up your hand before God and say:

"I decide right now before heaven and earth, before all the angels of God and all the demons of hell, that **I will be made whole.** I make a quality decision right now that **I will win and not lose.**"

"I base my decision on God's Word that says: *I pray that you will be fruitful in every good work* (Colossians 1:9,10); I am more than a conqueror through Christ Jesus Who loves me (Romans 8:37); This is the victory that overcomes the world, even our faith (I John 5:4); and that I should be of good cheer, because Jesus has overcome the world" (John 16:33).

"I have made my decision. **I will be made whole. Thank you, Father.**"

Be Determined To Win

Once you have made your decision, the manifestation may or may not come instantly. I have had several instant manifestations; but at other times I have had to stand on the Word of God for months before the manifestation came. That is where determination comes in.

The Greek word for *determined* means "a firmness of purpose." It also means "to give definite aim or direction; an unwavering resolution." Another definition for *determination* is "to set a boundary." Become determined: Set a boundary and don't compromise. Stay with the unwavering decision that you will be made whole.

When Jesus was talking about *wholeness,* He didn't confine or restrict the word to physical healing only. The word *healing* is not confined to the physical only; it is just another term for deliverance. Some marriages need to be made whole; they need healing. Some relationships need healing. Some people's finances need healing.

If you have any area in your life that needs healing spiritually, mentally, physically, or financially the Father God is asking, *Wilt thou be made whole?*

Make your decision. Answer yes to His question and become determined to back your decision.

Discipline and Diligence

To explain how to exercise discipline and diligence in achieving success, let me give you an example of how I obtained an airplane for my ministry.

I used to drive to all my speaking engagements; then the time came when the Spirit of God instructed me to believe for an airplane. When He told me that, I didn't know how to fly an airplane and neither did anyone on my staff. I thought, *Wouldn't I look like a jerk going down the highway at fifty-five miles per hour in a Cessna 310?*

But the Lord spoke to me and said, "Son, you are going to need an airplane in a few short days. Don't wait until the need becomes great. Get your faith out on the line now. Start now while you are not under pressure."

Someone may say, "I've never seen anything in the Word about airplanes!" I have! God said, *Delight thyself in the Lord; and I will cause thee to ride upon the high places of the earth* (Is. 58:14). Flying is riding the high places, isn't it?

After I learned that God's will for my ministry was to have an airplane, my staff and I began to believe the Lord for it.

I exercised the first two prerequisites:

I made the decision and became determined to win.

After we knew that it was the Lord's desire that we have the airplane, I made the decision that we would have it. Then I set a boundary. I made another decision that I was not going to use the world's system to get the airplane.

When you set a boundary and become determined to win, you have to let go of every alternate solution. You cannot say, "I can go this way to get what I want and if it doesn't work, I can always get it that way." As long as you think like that, you are not yet determined to win. You are planning to fail.

We made a decision, set a boundary line, and refused to cross over. We said, "In the name of Jesus, this is the way the airplane is going to come. We will not go any other way to get it."

Several months passed without the manifestation of an airplane. As my ministry expanded, I began conducting seminars all over the United States. The need for the airplane had arrived. I could not drive to all the places I needed to go.

My staff and I were still confessing the Word. I often flew with Charles Capps in his airplane, and as I did, I thanked the Lord for mine.

A year passed while I kept confessing the Word, but I saw no evidence of an airplane manifesting. No one came up to me and said, "Brother Jerry, the Lord told me to give you this money for an airplane." Not one quarter toward its purchase came in during that time, so I exercised the second two prerequisites - discipline and diligence.

I disciplined myself to speak the Word of God.

We kept confessing, "We will have that plane, in the name of Jesus."

One day when I was quiet before the Lord, He said to me, "Do you really believe that you will receive an airplane according to Mark 11:24?" (That verse says, *What things soever ye desire, when ye pray, believe that ye receive them, and ye shall have them.*)

"I certainly do," I said.

"Then why aren't you acting like it?"

"Lord, how in the world am I going to act like I have an airplane? Stand out on the runway? What would You do if You were in this situation? How would You act like You had an airplane?"

"Let Me ask you a question: How would it affect your schedule today if you had that airplane in the natural realm?"

"I could cover more territory. I could set up more meetings. I could go to more places where I am invited."

"That's right."

"Wait a minute! You are going to have to explain this in greater detail."

"Son, you can do one more thing to stretch your faith to its extreme. Set up your schedule as though you have an airplane. Set up such a tight schedule that the only way you can keep it is by flying. Don't break your word and don't cancel any meeting that you set up."

"Lord, do You know what that means? I'm traveling all over the United States now. If I set up my schedule like that, I will have to drive all night long."

In other words, I was saying, "Lord, what if it doesn't work?"

I had to discipline myself not to be moved by what I saw, felt, or heard.

I became diligent.

I began to discipline myself to call things that be not as though they were (Romans 4:17). I called the man who handled our scheduling and told him to write all the people throughout the United States who had invited me to come for meetings and tell them that I would come. I told him to book me up so tightly that there would be no other way for me to get there except to fly.

Even though he thought that I had lost my mind, he did what I asked him to do. He scheduled meetings in four different states within a seven day period. There was no way that I could drive from one meeting to the next.

When I looked at the schedule, I knew I had

to become very diligent; I could not afford to become lazy.

When the time came to go to those meetings, I had done everything except get out on the runway. I said, "Lord, I have a question. How am I going to get to all those meetings?"

He said, *"Fly!"*

I said, "But, Lord, I don't have an airplane."

"Fly the commercial airlines," He said.

"But, Lord, the commercial airlines don't service all the places I am scheduled to go."

He said, "You fly as far as you can and I will make the other arrangements. Every time you board an airplane, say, I am not moved by this. I am only moved by what I believe and I believe that I have my own airplane."

This is what my American Airlines ticket showed on my first trip: Fort Worth to Springfield, Missouri; Springfield to Columbia, South Carolina; Columbia to Los Angeles, California. I flew from one end of the country to the other. This kind of traveling went on for months, but I was determined to win.

Once as I was telling the ticket agent what kind of reservations I wanted, I heard something coming up on the inside of me. I knew that God was honoring His Word. At that moment, I didn't care who heard me as I said, "Sir, I just want you to know that I am not moved by this."

He said, "Pardon me?"

I said, "I want you to know that I am not moved by this. I believe that I have my own airplane in the name of Jesus."

"Yes, sir!" he said, "Gate number fourteen!"

As I boarded the airplane, I handed my ticket to the flight attendant and said, "Miss, I want you to know that I am not moved by this. I believe that I won't have to fly American Airlines much longer, in the name of Jesus, because I believe that I have my own airplane."

She said, "Yes, sir! Seat number two!"

Every time I looked out the window I could see myself, through the eye of faith, flying in my own airplane.

Six months went by. A total of a year and one-half had passed since I had started believing for my own airplane. During those six months, my schedule had been packed. One day while I was speaking at the Full Gospel Businessmen's Fellowship regional convention in Omaha, Nebraska, I received a phone call from my office manager informing me that some people in Dallas wanted to have dinner with me just as soon as I returned to Fort Worth.

When I arrived home, I called the man and made plans for my wife and me to meet him and some other people in Dallas for dinner. We met them and were enjoying our meal when the person seated next to me said, "We called this meeting because God has told us to give you an airplane."

When we left the restaurant that night, we had a time praising the Lord!

During the following year, we enjoyed flying from one end of the United States to the other in our Cessna 310. At the end of that time, the Lord said, "I want you to sell the airplane, take a portion of the money from the sale, and put it into other ministries. I want you to plant some seed. Son, there is coming a time in your ministry when the only way you can do the job that I want you to do is with a jet. I want you to start planting seeds *now*."

I obtained that airplane by using the four prerequisites. I made a decision to win and then backed it up with a firm resolution in my heart and mind that I was not going to compromise. I was not moved by what I saw, felt, or heard. I diligently made a steady and consistent effort to accomplish my goal.

Stand

I once heard a man say, "I am standing on the Word of God. If I fail, it is because the Word failed." The Word of God will not fail. The Bible says, *The grass withereth, the flower fadeth: but the word of our God shall stand for ever* (Isaiah 40:8).

Most people have been programmed all their lives to be moved by what they feel, see, and hear. Disci- pline can only come from the Word of God. Once you begin to discipline yourself, you will take an uncompromising stand. It will be God's way or no way at all.

Jesus said in John 8:31, *If ye continue in my word, then are ye my disciples indeed.* A disciple is a disciplined one. The Word of God is what disciplines you.

The Word of God will create discipline in you, enabling you to stand in the face of adverse circumstances and say, "I am not moved by what I see." Second Corinthians 4:18 says that what you see is temporal, or subject to change. The things that are seen are subject to change, but the Word of God is eternal. Not being moved by what you see, feel, or hear is the product of discipline.

Once you know what the Word says about the miracle you are seeking; once you exercise the prerequisites to success - decision, determination, discipline, and diligence - and are moved only by what the Word says, then you will win. God's Word works. You will receive the manifestation of the miracle.

How It Works

In the previous section, I gave you an example of how I used the four prerequisites for success to bring about the manifestation of a miracle in my life. Now I want to show you an example in God's Word of some New Testament men who used those same prerequisites to bring about the manifestation of a miracle.

We read in Luke 5:17-20:

And it came to pass on a certain day, as he (Jesus) was teaching, that there were Pharisees and doctors of the law sitting by, which were come out of every town of Galilee, and Judaea, and Jerusalem: and the power of the Lord was present to heal them.

And, behold, men brought in a bed a man which was taken with a palsy: and they sought means to bring him in, and to lay him before him.

And when they could not find by what way they might bring him in because of the multitude, they went upon the housetop, and let him down through the tiling with his couch into the midst before Jesus.

And when he saw their faith, he said unto him, Man, thy sins are forgiven thee.

It is evident that these men had heard about the ministry of Jesus, and what they heard created faith on the inside of them. These men believed that if they could get their friend into the presence of Jesus, he would be healed. But just knowing that was not enough. Many people know that God blesses, but they must make a decision to be blessed. They have to make a decision to be healed.

Perhaps the following took place: The two men were standing around talking about the ministry of Jesus when one said, "Did you see all those miracles that Jesus performed? Did you see Him cast out those evil spirits from those people who were possessed? Did you see the blind receive their sight and the deaf hear?" As they talked about the miracles of Jesus, they decided that their friend could be healed, too.

Decision

As they talked, the thought came to them, "If we can get our friend to that meeting, he could get healed of the palsy!" But just thinking about what could happen wasn't enough. They could have sat around all day talking about what could happen, but to no avail. For the condition to change, they had to make a decision to do something about it, so they went to the man's house.

He was lying on the couch, shaking uncontrollably because of the palsy. One of his friends said: "It won't be long now until you'll be whole. We're going to take you to Jesus and He will make you whole."

Their decision was made.

Determination

The two friends were determined to carry out their decision.

The sick man said, "Traveling to see Jesus would be a long trip and you would have to carry me. I don't think I am up to making such a journey."

His friends immediately responded, "We will get you there. Don't worry about anything. We are well able to carry you."

"I have had my hopes up many times only to be let down. I have had this disease all my life..."

"Quit relying on past experiences. We don't care about what has happened in the past. We just know that if we can get you into that meeting, you will be healed. Let's go."

"But I'm tired, boys. If God wants me healed, He'll just do it."

"You'll never get any better with that attitude. We know that if we get you to that meeting, you will be healed. And we are determined to get you there one way or another."

You may say, "That man's will was involved and he didn't agree with the decision."

That's right, but if you keep telling a person the Good News, you can change his mind. The only reason a person wills not to choose Jesus, is that his mind has been blinded from seeing the truth of the Gospel (2 Corinthians 4:4). If you keep telling him the Good News, you can get the blinders off his mind by the glorious light of the Gospel.

The men kept telling the sick man that he would be healed until he, too, believed. Then off they went on their trip. It was a long journey, but they were determined to win.

Finally, they arrived at the house where Jesus was preaching. People were standing everywhere. The place was full. No one would let them go inside. At this point, it looked as though they had wasted a trip.

Discipline

These men were not moved by what they saw. They saw that the crowd would not let them in.

They were not moved by what they heard. The

Bible doesn't record every conversation that went on in that particular scene, but people in those days were just like people are today. They spoke many negative things.

These men were not moved by what they felt. One of them said to the man standing in the doorway: "Please help us, sir. This man has the palsy, and we have carried him a long way to get him into this meeting." But the man ignored them.

The sick man, worn out from the trip, was getting discouraged. He said, "Let's go home. I appreciate what you've done, but if it had been God's will to heal me, He would have opened the door."

But his friends said, "Hush that kind of talk. Just lie there and praise God for your healing. We brought you up here to get you healed, and we are not leaving until you are."

"What are we going to do?"

They scratched their heads and said, "Maybe we can get in through a window." They walked around the house and checked every window, but people were sitting in them.

Diligence

Remember, the Bible says that when they could not get in, *they sought means.* That word 'means' is plural. When you are determined to win, you will seek means. They were not going to quit until they won.

As they kept on ministering to their sick friend, they sought means whereby they could get him to Jesus. Finally, they said, "Let's ask God to show us a way to get into this place. There has to be a way."

Suddenly, their faces lit up. "Let's climb on the roof. There's nobody up there!"

The sick man said, "Wait a minute! I appreciate your sincerity, but you are not taking me up on the roof. I have the palsy now, but if I fall off that roof, I will really be in bad shape!"

They encouraged their friend: "Don't worry. We are going to carry you up there, rip out some shingles, and lower you down into the room where Jesus is."

They refused to quit trying and somehow got their friend on the roof. Jesus was preaching the Word when He looked up and saw the two men lower their sick friend into the room. Jesus stopped in the middle of what He was saying. When the couch was lowered to the floor, Jesus turned to the sick man and said, "Take up your bed and walk!" Immediately, the man walked (Luke 5:24,25).

This is an example of winning at its best. These men exercised the prerequisites that lead to victory and success.

They made a **decision** to win and started on their trip with the **determination** to do so. When they reached their destination, **discipline** took charge. Those people had every adverse circumstance come against them, just as you and I do today, but they were not moved by what they saw, heard, or felt. Through diligence, they made a steady and consistent effort to accomplish a miracle.

When Jesus *saw their faith*, He healed the man with the palsy.

Can Jesus see your faith? Faith is what activates God.

Do you need a miracle? **Make your decision** now to get it. **Be determined** that you will win. **Discipline yourself** to think, speak, and do only what the Word says. **Be diligent** - never give up.

Once you have done these things, victory and success are yours!

Dr. Jerry Savelle is a noted author, evangelist, and teacher who travels extensively throughout the United States, Canada, and around the globe. He is president of Jerry Savelle Ministries International, a ministry of many outreaches devoted to meeting the needs of believers all over the world.

Well-known for his balanced Biblical teaching, Dr. Savelle has conducted seminars, crusades and conventions for over twenty-five years and has ministered in thousands of churches and fellowships. He is in great demand today because of his inspiring message of victory and faith and his vivid, and often humorous, illustrations from the Bible. He teaches the uncompromised Word of God with a power and an authority that is exciting, but with a love that delivers the message directly to the spirit man.

In addition to his international headquarters in Crowley, Texas, Dr. Savelle is also founder of JSMI Africa, JSMI United Kingdom, JSMI South Africa and JSMI Tanzania. In 1994, he established the JSMI Bible Institute and School of World Evangelism. It is a two-year school for the preparation of ministers to take the Gospel of Jesus Christ to the nations of the world.

The missions outreach of his ministry extends to over 50 countries around the world. JSMI further ministers the Word of God through its prison ministry outreach.

Dr. Savelle has authored many books and has an extensive video and cassette teaching tape ministry and a nation-wide television broadcast. Thousands of books, tapes, and videos are distributed around the world each year through Jerry Savelle Ministries International.

For a complete list of tapes, videos, and books by Jerry Savelle, write:

Jerry Savelle Ministries International
P. O. Box 748
Crowley, TX 76036

Feel free to include your prayer requests and comments when you write.